3

'6.2

MW01121419

DATE DUE

OCT 2 6 2010		OCT 1 4 2010
NOV 2 9 2013		DEC 0 2 2013

KILT

KiLt

by Jonathan Wilson

PLAYWRIGHTS CANADA PRESS
Toronto • Canada

Kilt © Copyright by Jonathan Wilson, 1998

Playwrights Canada Press
54 Wolseley Street, 2nd Floor
Toronto, Ontario CANADA M5T 1A5
(416) 703-0201   fax (416) 703-0059
cdplays@interlog.com   http://www.puc.ca

Playwrights Canada Press acknowledges the support of The Canada Council for the Arts for our publishing programme, and the Ontario Arts Council.

*Cover design by Tony Hamill. Playwright photo by Tim Leyes.
Cover photo by Cylla Von Tiedemann - Paul Braunstein in the Tarragon Theatre production, Toronto, 1999.*

Canadian Cataloguing in Publication Data

Wilson, Jonathan
    Kilt

A play.
ISBN 0-88754-583-1

I. Title.
PS8595.I58342K54 1999   jC812'.54   C99-932598-1
PR9199.3.W49845K54 1999

First printing - January 2000
Printed and bound by Hignell Printing at Winnipeg, MB, Canada.

Jonathan Wilson started writing with The Second City, Toronto, collaborating as a writer and performer on six shows. He has written two one-act plays, ".43 Calibre Testing" and "Beyond the Purple Sunrise". He wrote the script for the National Film Board short film "Funeral Games" and worked as a sketch writer on the CBC comedy pilots "Love Sex and Other Natural Disasters" and "In Through the Out Door". His one-man show, "My Private Oshawa" had an extended run in Toronto and was nominated for a Dora Mavor Moore Award and a Chalmers Award. "Kilt" had an extended run at Tarragon Theatre in Toronto and was nominated for seven Dora Mavor Moore Awards, including Best New Play. His new play, "Well", is now being developed at Tarragon Theatre, and he will be appearing in the Toronto production of "The Lion King" as Timon.

Kilt
is dedicated to the memory of my father
James Maurice Wilson

ACKNOWLEDGMENTS

"Kilt" was developed in workshops and readings at Tarragon Theatre (actors: Maja Ardal, Paul Braunstein, Jillian Cook, Mary Francis Moore, Christopher Morris, Deborah Lambie, Gerard Parkes, Jordan Pettle, Shaun Smyth, Brendan Wall; dramaturgs: Andy McKim, Urjo Kareda); at The Shaw Festival (actors: Neil Barclay, Jo-Anne Kirwan Clark, Deborah Lambie, Jennifer Phipps, Mike Shara; dramaturg: Ed Sahely); and at the 1998 Banff play*Rites* Colony (actors: Maja Ardal, Lindsay Burns, Ken Kramer, Grant Linneberg, Antony Santiago; dramaturgs: Joanna McIntyre, Andy McKim).

Thanks also to Laurie Lynd and Ed Sahely who started on this road with me.

"Kilt" opened at Tarragon Theatre, Toronto, in April, 1999.

Directed by Andy McKim.
Set & lighting designed by Stephen Droege.
Costumes designed by Sue LePage.
Sound designed by John Gzowski.
Choreographer — Joyce Kite.
Assistant Director — Mary Francis Moore.
Stage manager — Maria Costa.

CAST

CAPTAIN LAVERY	*Brendan Wall*
MAC and TOM	*Paul Braunstein*
ESTHER	*Maja Ardal*
MARY	*Deborah Lambie*
DAVID	*Gerard Parkes*

PLAYWRIGHT'S NOTES

This play was born when I saw a photograph of two Scottish soldiers in an embrace in the desert in North Africa during World War II From there, it became my challenge to give them a history and life. And now, here they are frozen in time. This work is only possible due to the support and encouragement of everyone at Tarragon Theatre. Andy McKim and Urjo Kareda gave me a chance to make a leap forward as a writer and I can't thank them enough. Thanks also to my family and friends who encouraged me during the writing of the play. Up yer kilt!

THE CHARACTERS

TOM	early twenties, exotic Highland dancer
MAC	early twenties, a working-class Private from Glasgow
ESTHER	early 50s, Highland Dance teacher
MARY	late 40s, housewife
DAVID	early seventies, a gentleman from Edinburgh
LAVERY	Early twenties, an upper-class Captain from Edinburgh

THE SETTING

North Africa, 1941; Hamilton, Toronto, and Glasgow, Scotland in the present.

For the original production, the set was a series of small hills or dunes that, with the addition of simple props and lighting, facilitated the various locations.

ACT ONE

Midnight. Tobruk - the north desert in Libya, 1941. A British army camp. Peaceful other than the sounds of distant voices, laughter and a scratchy record playing George Formby singing "Fanlight Fanny".

In half light, MAC, a young soldier dressed in a regimental kilt, military shirt and cap, smokes and keeps watch . LAVERY, a young captain, comes to the edge of the light and watches MAC silently for a while. He wears military kahkis shorts and shirt. He smiles then breaks the silence.

LAVERY   Can I get a fag?

A startled MAC looks. After a start, he sees it's LAVERY.

MAC   Bloody hell! Captain Lavery! You scared the shite outta me.

LAVERY   That was the point.

MAC   Ya wee prick! Uh ... sir.

LAVERY   Stand easy, Private McPhail.

MAC   Well thank you, sir.

MAC salutes then hands LAVERY a cigarette

MAC   Here yi go.

               MAC gives him a cigarette and lights it for him.

LAVERY   Thank you, Private.

               They both smoke.

LAVERY   So, McPhail. No surprise attacks tonight?

MAC   No, sir. Well, Rommel did stop by earlier but I told him to come back when we were better prepared.

LAVERY   Good work. The regiment's safety is in your very capable hands, Private. We are all counting on you.

MAC   Thank you, Captain. I shall do my best to uphold my duty.

LAVERY   Good.

               Silence.

MAC   Are they still celebratin?

LAVERY   Yes, Private.

MAC   Hell you'd think they'd won the war wi' that racket. What's a' the fuss?

LAVERY   A small celebration. General Donaldson is very pleased. We've held off any German advance for over a month. No shelling for three nights. For now Tobruk is ours.

MAC   Aye. Who' the hell'd want it?

	Silence.
LAVERY	Mac, I wanted to make sure you were awake. I overheard Corporal Lancaster ordering surprise inspections.
MAC	The now?
LAVERY	What better time to catch lollygaggers?
MAC	Ah Christ! That's all I need.
	MAC quickly puts out his cigarette.
LAVERY	Not to worry. I volunteered And all seems in order.
MAC	I did nearly kip off half an 'our ago. I thought I was back hame... I thought I cou' hear my Da cawin' ta me. I was late for the docks ... the cart had to be loaded up wi fish ... and I forgot. I think I'm going a wee bit daft.
LAVERY	That's nay surprise to me.
	LAVERY leans in and kisses MAC. MAC is willing at first them pushed him away. He stands and looks to see if they are still alone.
MAC	Ya sly bastard, David. Have you no shame?
LAVERY	I thought that's what you liked about me?
MAC	No, the now! Wha' if Donaldson walked up right then?
LAVERY	I'd have to say "Sir ... this Private is spoken for but I'm sure Sergeant Davis, so captivating as Marlene Dietrich in last night's Easter pageant, would be more

than willing."

MAC   (*laughs*) He would be too...

LAVERY   I wanted to see what it felt like without
               being drunk.

MAC   And?

LAVERY   Lovely.

MAC   Yes. And you have had a whiskey ya
               lucky bastard. I can taste it on ya.

LAVERY   Just a dram.

                    He moves in close to MAC.

LAVERY   Now don't be such a big lassie! We've
               been safe before. No one comes back
               here.

MAC   Aye. Except me.

LAVERY   And me sometimes. If someone finds us,
               we just pretend that we're...

MAC   I know. We just pretend we're fighting.

LAVERY   Wrestling! That's what we did at my
               school.

MAC   Aye ... easy fer you. They'd look the other
               way wi you. It'd be off ta the cracker bin
               fer me. We agreed to meet the 'morra
               night.

LAVERY   I know. I'm being greedy.

MAC   Yes. Very much so, Captain. You're terri-
               ble. If you are not careful you will find
               yourself on warning.

> *MAC leans in and kisses LAVERY. A sound startles LAVERY.*

LAVERY   No.

MAC   Wha'?

LAVERY   You're right. We should be patient.

MAC   Aye! Yer a big tease!

> *Silence.*

LAVERY   Look at that sky. Brilliant. I hated this bloody place when I first got here.

MAC   Aye, I remember. Now look at ya. Only a month and yer Sahib a' the bloody desert.

LAVERY   Yes. I'm feeling more at home. I mean think of Edinburgh. Miserable. No mystery there. You and I should grab a few spare camels and head into the night... "The Arabian Nights".

MAC   The what?

LAVERY   Christ, Mac! Have you no read a book in yer life?

MAC   The Bible ... twice. And besides I'm heading back to Glasgow. It's full 'a mystery.

LAVERY   I guess you could call it that.

MAC   It's funny what the desert will make a man do.

LAVERY   Yes, Private. It must be the heat. I hope you'll write when we get back...?

MAC   I'm no one for letters, David.

LAVERY   No. Come up and see me. A weekend at the University.

MAC   I just might. You're invited to the wedding if you can get away from your books.

LAVERY   I'd get to meet the lovely Rose?

MAC   She is lovely. You'd get on fine.

The sound of a piper at the celebration can be heard in the distance. It plays to the end of the scene.

MAC   The pipes are calling you, sir. Ye should gie back ta the do.

LAVERY   Yes.

Silence.

LAVERY   I had a wee dream about you last night, Private.

MAC   Really?

LAVERY   Yes. You were dancing the highland fling ... on a beautiful sunny day in the hills back home.

MAC   Was I? Lucky me.

LAVERY   Oh yes.

MAC   Where were you?

LAVERY   Sitting at your feet. Clapping to the music.

MAC   Lovely.

Silence.

LAVERY	Well, Private. I'm off to my kip.
MAC	Yes, sir.
LAVERY	Be on the lookout.

> *LAVERY exits. MAC does a small fling. He smiles and then dances again. The distant sound of the bagpipes grows louder. His dance becomes wilder and wilder and MAC removes his shirt. The pipe music becomes more intense then it is overtaken as heavy dance music kicks in and the lighting shifts to suggest a strip club in present day Toronto. MAC is now TOM a dancer. He is just reaching the finale of his combination strip and highland dance routine.*
> *We hear feedback from a microphone then an announcer speaks.*

MC	(*voice over*) All righty!! That was Tartan Tom! Yeah! Tom is our senior dancer here at The Ranch and he just gets better with every year.

> *A single pair of hands claps with one whistle.*

TOM	Thanks.
MC	Remember all of our dancers are available upstairs for a hot and steamy private table dance...

> *TOM picks up his shirt from the stage and yells towards the announcer.*

TOM	Yeah. If I don't fucking quit. Mike! Are you listening to me? I told you to crank my music. I could hear the fucking toilet flush. It affects tips. I've been keeping track.

Mike?

MC   And remember it's two dances for one
      Tuesday. Don't forget to get yourself a
      cocktail and ... please ... welcome to the
      main stage ... gentlemen and gentlemen...
      Tristan.

TOM   Amateur!

      *A man enters and takes a seat. TOM
      approaches him.*

TOM   Hi there. Would you like a fling?

      *The man nods. TOM dances for the man
      on a small box in front of him.*

      *The music stops. TOM still dances.
      ESTHER ROBERTSON enters to
      address her class.*

ESTHER Good morning, everyone.

      Silence.

      I'm Mrs. Robertson.

      Thank you.

      Let me take this opportunity to welcome
      you all to the Premiere level classes here
      at the Robertson Royal Academy of
      Highland Dancing for Hamilton-
      Wentworth.

      Quite.

      Oh. uh ... yes, my compliments to Mr.
      Singh and Miss Bonapiel for putting
      together this morning's tea and ... uh ...
      bagels. Just lovely.

ESTHER	As we all know, renovations are complete and, due to the expansion of the Tae Kwon Doe studio next door, we have lost half of our class space and we now occupy only one third of the second floor here at the Crossroads Mini-Mall. But the school shall survive. And we will bravely soldier on into our twentieth year.

Very exciting.

A single set of hands clap.

ESTHER	Thank you, Mr. Singh.

The man tries to put his hand up TOM's kilt.

TOM	No buddy. Sorry. No touching. Not tonight. Don't worry, you'll get a show.
ESTHER	Now, to work. We have only got six months until the world championships in Dunoon, Scotland and I expect you all to be vying for a spot. Unfortunately, as of yet, only one student from the school has even risen to the National levels. But hope springs.

All you have to remember is that this work is not to be interpreted but lived up to. The sooner you accept that the sooner we can get about the business of removing the bad habits that I see infecting your work.

This morning's presentation in sword dancing for example. Horrifying. It was personally disturbing for me to see some of the young ladies taking liberties with their legs. Do you feel you can fly in the face of a thousand years of tradition with an extra flick of your toe?

She zeros in on a student.

ESTHER   I'm talking to you Miss Chan! Smiling and grimacing through your work like you were dancing with your face. Neutral!

And please remember, Miss Kolinsky. The kilt brushes the knee. It does not fully cover. It does not fully reveal. It brushes!

She sees another student.

ESTHER   Oh yes. It's nice to see a new face here at The Academy. You should know class, our new student is an award winner at the provincial level.

Isn't that right?

Well let me take this opportunity to say on behalf of the whole school that this holds absolutely no weight with me, Duncan Tate. You are my student now and I will assume you know nothing. I don't mean to be harsh, Mr. Tate. Let me assure you that although I am a demanding task master I can also be a trusted confidant and have been known to laugh quite freely.

If you are here to study Highland dance then I welcome you with open arms ... if you are here in some misguided attempt to twist this work to your own whims then I respectfully ask you to pack up your locker and take up the accordion! Anyone?

Silence.

Good.

> *The man whispers to TOM.*

ESTHER   This work is about control.

> *The man hands TOM a pill.*

TOM   Well look at that.

ESTHER   And precision.

> *TOM swallows the pill.*

TOM   Complete ecstasy.

> *The man whispers again to TOM. They exit together.*

ESTHER   A word of warning students. I once saw a selfish dancer get entangled in her own ego. Not a pretty sight. She was building to her final spring point and brought her foot out with a ... flourish! That's all it took. Her foot swept into the saber below relieving her of the top of her big toe. Now, as we know, sharpened swords are no longer allowed for competition and great is the loss. I call on all of you in the work ahead to believe that you are dancing over razors.

Let's have a wonderful and productive first day.

From the top, Mr. Singh. And please keep your improvisations to yourselves.

> *The lights shift revealing TOM in bed slowly awakening. Beside him asleep is the man from the club. TOM looks at him and remembers the night before.*

TOM   Oh, yeah.

TOM pokes at the man until he stirs.

TOM   Shit, sorry. Morning buddy. Did I wake you?

             The man starts to answer. TOM stops him.

TOM   Shhh. Let's not spoil it.

             The telephone rings.

TOM   You should get going.

             Ring. The man starts to dress. The answering machine picks up.

TOM   (*on the answering machine*) Tom and Marco! Go.

             BEEEEEEEEEEP!

ESTHER   (*on machine*) Hello? Thomas. It's Mrs. Robertson. It's your Mum.

TOM   Kill me.

ESTHER   Hello? Thomas? Are you there? No. Well anyway ... I thought I'd try you again. Maybe you didn't get the twelve messages yesterday. If you're dead ... it would be nice if you let me know. If you're not ... I was wondering about Easter. Are you coming home?

             Yes or no?

             Yes. That's all.

             I'll hang up now.

             The man picks up the phone and hands it to TOM.

ESTHER	ꓱello?

TOM looks at the phone in horror.

TOM	What are you doing?

He takes the phone.

ESTHER	Thomas? Are you there? Hello? I can hear breathing.

He talks into the phone.

TOM	Yeah. Hi.
ESTHER	Oh ... hello. It's your Mum.
TOM	Yeah ... I know.

Silence.

TOM	Uh ... how are you?
ESTHER	Oh ... the same.
TOM	Right.

The man goes down on TOM. He moans.

TOM	Ahhh.
TOM	(*to man*) No.
ESTHER	Are you getting a cold?

TOM pushes the man's head away.

TOM	No! I'm fine.
ESTHER	Well you're definitely getting a haunted look. I noticed it the last time I saw you. It's a year ago next month, ya know? You were the colour of ash. You used to

be so rosy cheeked. It's working in that damn bar. You've become a vampire. A bartender? Oh Tom. What was wrong with the Starbucks, hmm?

TOM   I make more tips bartending.

ESTHER   Tips? Is that what we're reduced to? That's not why we came to Canada.

TOM   We're not refugees.

                The man is ready to leave. He gives TOM some money.

TOM   Jesus. It was a freebie!

                The man exits.

ESTHER   What? Is someone there?

TOM   No.

ESTHER   Oh dear God. Yes. Well ... all I wanted to know was ... are you maybe coming home for Easter? You know — Bunnies. Chocolate.

TOM   What? You've gotta be kidding.

ESTHER   I don't see the humour.

TOM   Ya know ... I'm not really up to any Easter egg hunts this year.

ESTHER   I found some new hiding places.

TOM   No.

ESTHER   Oh, I see. Christmas, Hogmanay, Robbie Burns day, your birthday — now this.

TOM   I have to hang up now.

ESTHER   No. I finally catch you in and I get the bums rush? No.

          I was thinking of you all morning. A wee bubble came into my head. It was our first day back at The Academy. Oh Tom ... what a sorry lot. Only one boy in the whole class and definitely lacking in your natural ability. You know you're not too old to start again.

TOM   DON'T!

ESTHER   Sorry.

TOM   I've got to go.

ESTHER   No! Tom?

TOM   What?

ESTHER   Uh ... well ... uh ... how are you?

TOM   How am I?

ESTHER   Yes. How are things?

TOM   Oh no. I don't think we should play today.

ESTHER   I want to know. I'm asking.

TOM   Oh you're asking, are ya? What brings this on?

ESTHER   I'm feeling strong today. I had an Al Pacino coffee for breakfast.

TOM   An Al... ? Look, I'm fine. I'm alive. Let's just leave it at that. It's safer.

ESTHER   No! I want to know.

TOM	Oh. Alright, Mrs. Robertson. Okay. How am I? How are things? Well let's see. Okay. Well ... Marco left.
ESTHER	Oh no.
TOM	Yeah.
ESTHER	Who?
TOM	Marco. We've been together almost a year. I tried to tell you about him once.
ESTHER	Oh yes.
TOM	Yes.
ESTHER	Oh well, another one, eh?
TOM	Yeah. Apparently I'm high maintenance.
ESTHER	Well, there's a surprise. Sorry. So?
TOM	So I'm a little DEPRESSED! OKAY?
ESTHER	Oh depressed, are ya? You need a kick in the arse, that's all you need.
TOM	And she's off.
ESTHER	When I was your age we didn't have time for depression. You just got on with it. Just get on with it.
TOM	(*imitating her*) just get on with it! I am for ... fuck's sake!
ESTHER	LANGUAGE! And don't mock me.
TOM	Mock mock mock!

ESTHER	Let's just stop there.
TOM	Oh that's it? That's the line?
ESTHER	Yes.
TOM	Why did you even ask?
ESTHER	I don't know. Temporary insanity. Oh bloody hell. What a life. Do you think it's easy to be me?
TOM	No. I would imagine it's very difficult.
ESTHER	Yes, well it is. In my position. With you and your twists and turns. I'm still adjusting to you being a wee bit off.
TOM	I told you when I was twelve.
ESTHER	Yes well ... I make it a point never to believe a twelve-year old.

Oh if you just kept it to yourself. It's like you all want your own parade. Oh remember Mrs. Gate's son, Adam.? |
TOM	Yes.
ESTHER	Yes, well ... he's come out of the cupboard, you see.
TOM	There's a surprise.
ESTHER	Yes.

What?

Oh.

I met his Mum at this support group. English, Scottish, Irish, and Welsh parents of your kind and the trans-engineered |

other ones.

TOM   Trans...? Oh. You went?

ESTHER   Yes. It was posted at the Dominion.

TOM   I would pay to see that.

ESTHER   Well I'm not going back. Oh they're so
                   optimistic at first. She still thinks it means
                   her son will take her to the opera and
                   help her pick drapes. Have I got news for
                   her.

                   Silence.

ESTHER   Hello?

TOM   Yeah.

ESTHER   Oh smile for God's sake. What's to
                   become of you Tom? Oh if your dad was
                   alive he'd soon have you at the
                   University. Studying. Expanding your
                   mind. Oh Tom think about it. Yer no
                   spring chicken ya know?

TOM   I know.

ESTHER   For your dad, Tom. He'd be so proud. A
                   place in the world.

                   So I'll see you on Sunday? I'm making
                   blood pudding.

TOM   You're making blood?

ESTHER   It's your favourite.

TOM   I've gotta go.

                   TOM hangs up. Click.

ESTHER   Hello?

                    TOM counts the money.

TOM   No tip.

ESTHER   Hello.

                    *TOM stands. He is already dressed in his
                    kilt. He puts on a shirt and dresses for his
                    sword dance.*

ESTHER   Hello? Tom. Thomas Robertson?
                    If you've hung up I'll...

                    Tom?

                    She hangs up.

ESTHER   I don't know where he gets it.

                    Dance music. A voice over in the club.

MC   Remember all our dancers are available
                    for a hot hot hot private table dance
                    upstairs. Go on. Enjoy.

                    *TOM starts doing feverish push ups
                    pumping up to dance.*

                    *The music cuts out except for a thumping
                    bass. Lights tight on TOM's head.*

TOM   Shit. My head.

                    I shouldn't have gotten so fucked up last
                    night.

                    It feels like dust.

                    A desert in my brain.

                    The lighting shifts to the desert in intense

*midday sun. The sound of trucks. It is
now MAC doing push ups. Young LAV-
ERY enters carrying an overstuffed duffel
bag. He crosses in front of MAC, stops
turns back, and their eyes meet.*

LAVERY   Oh ... uh ... hello.

MAC   Hallo.

*MAC smiles then turns his face away
and continues his push ups. LAVERY
exits. The lights crash back to the club.
Loud music of the club and the lighting
shifts back to the club. It is TOM again.
Did he just see LAVERY? He shakes it
off.*

MC   Now please welcome to the stage an old,
               old, old ... old favourite of ours..

TOM   YOU FUCK!

MC   ...TARTAN TOM!

*A dance version of Andy Stewart singing
"Donald Where's Your Troosers" plays.
TOM enters on stage carrying his two
swords. He crosses them on the floor and
he starts into a traditional sword dance,
leaping higher and higher with each turn.
TOM continues to dance and takes off his
shirt as the dance becomes more sexual.*

*We see ESTHER weave her way through
the club. She stops dead in her tracks
when she sees TOM.*

ESTHER   Thomas Robertson!

TOM stops dancing and looks down.

ESTHER   What have you done now?

TOM	What the hell are you doing here?

ESTHER turns to the crowd.

ESTHER	Avert your eyes! Avert your eyes!

TOM runs to her as she flees the club. TOM catches up to her as the club sounds fade. ESTHER turns looks at TOM and swoons.

ESTHER	Oh!
TOM	Shit! Are you ... are you gonna...?
ESTHER	No.

TOM runs to her and she falls into his arms, a tight spot on her face.

ESTHER   Oh damn. I've passed out. Yes.

It's how I'm able to have this wee moment to myself.

Well, he's finally done it. He's killed me. What was it that turned him? The feeling of the kilt against his knees? My Shirley Bassey records? He would sing along. I don't know. I can't be held responsible.

It's a mystery.

I grew suspicious around his ninth birthday. Coburg Highland Games. Watching him dance the Seann Triubhas. The smile on his face. It's a beautiful dance commemorating the return of the wearing of the kilt to Scotland. It celebrates the removal of one's trousers. It was always his favourite.

What a life. As you get older you learn to

accept that thing are not going to blossom and bloom as you wish they would.

Oh I could do with a wee cuppa tea.

In real time she has only passed out for a few seconds. She rejoins the living.

ESTHER   Oh. Somebody kill me!

She flees the club, TOM in tow.

TOM   Just try to calm down.

ESTHER   Get away from me.

MC   That was Tartan Tom ... and the ugliest drag queen I have ever seen! Now please welcome to the mainstage ... Alonzo.

ESTHER finds herself in an alley behind the club. The sound of traffic horns etc. The thump of the club is still felt like a heart beat.

ESTHER   Where am I?

TOM   Just try and calm down!

ESTHER   I will not calm down! Getaway from me ... you wee bastard!

TOM   What are you doing here?

ESTHER   Dear God! Tell me someone's holding you against your will, Tom.

TOM   No.

ESTHER   Is it some kind of cult? Have they got ya hopped up on the heroin?

TOM   No no no. I'm fine.

ESTHER	Yes I guess you are. Not too depressed to take your clothes off for strangers are you?
TOM	How did you find this place?
ESTHER	You left a pack of matches at the house.

She produces the matches and reads from the cover.

ESTHER	The Ranch!

She throws the matches at TOM.

ESTHER	I thought it was a steak house.
TOM	Yeah well .... all beef all the time.
ESTHER	Disgusting! You know I think I've been a pretty good sport with everything you get up to but this is a little hard to take. To be forced by a man dressed as Anne Murray to pay ten dollars to see that. Oh if your wee friends in the Pipe Band could see you now!
TOM	Yeah well I suggest you don't tell them.
ESTHER	It's like you're trying to shock me on purpose so I'll crack.
TOM	Now don't flatter yourself.
ESTHER	Oh that's nice. I'm not even worth the effort.
TOM	Sometimes ... I think maybe you crave it Mrs. Robertson. My, my, what a dull day here at The Royal Academy. I think I'll call on Tom for a wee afternoon shock." "Tom how are things? Oh my!"

ESTHER   I can't be shocked anymore, Tom. You've robbed me of that.

TOM   Look ... I admit this probably doesn't look good ... but I'm just dancing. I'm just...

ESTHER   Dancing? I saw you Tom! Your lovely sword dance all perverted in that way! In your Granda's kilt!

Oh Tom. I didn't come to ambush you. He's dead.

TOM   Who?

ESTHER   Mac. My Da's deed ... Old Mac's deed.

TOM   Shit.

ESTHER   Yes. Your Auntie Mary called during Wheel of Fortune.

Just went off to sleep on the settee. Mary had made him a nice supper and then he ... left. Poor soul.

TOM   How's Auntie Mary?

ESTHER   Oh, a simpleton as usual. She was sobbin' so hard on the phone I could barely understand her. "Ohhh I'm all alone in the hoose. I don't know what ta do." I'm going back to Scotland to see it's done proper. My flight leaves in three hours. When I went to pick up my air tickets something very strange happened. I bought one for you.

                                 Silence from TOM. She takes a small parcel out of her purse and hands it to him.

ESTHER   Yer Granda sent a present for your birthday. It just arrived today. Brylcream and a pack of cards. He knows you're a man now.

TOM   I.... I ... don't know.

ESTHER   No, of course not. I wouldn't think about dragging you away from all this.

TOM   I never even met him.

ESTHER   You selfish bugger! You did so. You knew him' til you were three months old. He called you Bubble.

            Tom?

            Silence from TOM. ESTHER grabs for the kilt.

ESTHER   I should have known better. Right! Give me his kilt.

TOM   What?

ESTHER   Give me his kilt! I want him buried in it.

TOM   No. You said he wanted me to have it.

ESTHER   Yes. Well that's not important now is it? Give it to me, Tom.

TOM   I don't have any pants.

ESTHER   I'm sure that won't bother you.

TOM   I can't go. We would kill each other.

ESTHER   Don't say that.

TOM   I don't think you get it. We don't like each other. You go. They don't even know me.

ESTHER	No. And what a pretty picture you are. Showin yer whacker to the world. You know what they would have called you back in Glasgow?
	A skanky tart. Well that's what you are.
TOM	Yeah. Exactly. So go alone. You said there was only one way you would take me back there. Remember? As the star student. Goin for the gold. And ... I mean this is not exactly the world championships.
ESTHER	No. If you hadn't dropped out at the Nationals we would have gone for the Worlds in Scotland. You would have won.
TOM	I don't care. I didn't care.
ESTHER	No you didn't. Day of the finals. A case of nerves as I remember it.
	Well you've certainly got a nerve now!
TOM	Here I dance for myself. It has nothing to do with you.
ESTHER	Are you blind?
TOM	It's been six years! It's mine now.
	I dance at The Ranch. So what? It's a skill applied. Thank's to our lack of foresight it's the only real skill I have.
ESTHER	Oh yes, you're right, Tom. It's my fault you're a stripper.
TOM	Exotic entertainer.
ESTHER	Don't kid yourself.

TOM	It's just like when I was in competition. My number pinned to my skirt.
ESTHER	Kilt!
TOM	Whatever... Checking out the other dancers. The judges watching my every move. Points given at the end. Every god damn Highland Games in Eastern Canada. Packed up in the van. Rehearsing at the side of highways at truck stops.
	The only difference is you not being down front reminding me not to smile. You should be proud. I'm carrying on the tradition.
ESTHER	Proud? You've no shame, Tom.
TOM	Not as much as you'd like, I guess.
ESTHER	No.

Silence.

ESTHER	Tom, please.
	I don't ask much. It's just for three days. You have to be there. He was a war hero. There has to be the proper amount of respect.

Silence.

ESTHER	You owe me.

Silence. She grabs for the kilt again.

TOM	No. Don't. I'll wear it. I'll come.
ESTHER	You will?

TOM	Yeah.
ESTHER	Oh, thank God. Why?
TOM	I don't know.
ESTHER	Yes well ... don't think about it too much. We came here a team and that's how we'll go back.
TOM	Yeah.
ESTHER	Right. We've to get to the airport. Let's get the hell out of here.
	Oh Tom?
TOM	Yes?
ESTHER	When we're home, I need you to try to be my sweet lad. You know — the other one. Understand?
TOM	Yes.
ESTHER	We have to let them know that things worked out all right. Be my rosy-cheeked sweet lad.
TOM	I'll do my best.
	Silence.
TOM	I'm sorry.
ESTHER	What?
TOM	Your Dad ... Granda.
ESTHER	Oh yes. Well ... these things happen.
TOM	Should we hug?

ESTHER   Maybe later.

                The lighting shifts as ESTHER exits.
                TOM stands for a beat.

                The lighting shifts to the desert, 1942, a
                burning midday sun. The sound of a jeep
                passing, general hubbub CAPTAIN
                LAVERY enters looking a little lost, car-
                rying a duffel bag. MAC spots him,
                comes down front and salutes.

LAVERY   Private?

MAC   Yes, sir?

LAVERY   Are you Private McPhail?

MAC   Yes, sir. That's me, sir. Ah hell, are you
                Captain Lavery?

LAVERY   Yes, Private.

MAC   Really?

LAVERY   Yes. Private. Is there a problem? I was
                told you would show me to my quarters.

MAC   Aye, sir, right Yes. I was ta let ya know
                the stack tent was repaired, sir.

LAVERY   Yes? Thank you.

MAC   Yes, sir, it's repaired the now, sir. Every
                rip is now closed and the quarters are
                ready for your occupancy. Just behind the
                ridge here, sir. Welcome ta Tobruk, sir.

LAVERY   Oh yes. Well thank you, Private. Just
                behind the ridge?

MAC   Yes, sir. I'll tak yer kit, sir. Is this a', sir.

LAVERY   For now. My trunk's to follow.

MAC   I'll see ya get it as soon as it arrives sir.

LAVERY   Thank you, Private.

MAC   Just follow me. Careful now. Watch no scruff yer boots.

They travel a distance.

MAC   Ya must a' had quite the journey in sir.

LAVERY   Oh yes. Three days at sea.

MAC   I hear the harbours a shootin' match most days.

LAVERY   Yes. Not much choice. Being boxed in as you are on all sides.

MAC   Well yer on dry land the now, sir. Hae ya had the grand tour yet?

LAVERY   No. Not yet.

MAC   Right. Well we've spread oot a bit. The mess is oer' in the auld school. Officers mess further up near the kirk ... .and ya can smell yer way ta the privy.

They travel towards the tent.

LAVERY   Uh ... McPhail

MAC   Sir?

DAVID   How long have you been here?

MAC   Oe'r two years, sir. Landed in Alexandria on tae Libya o'er tae Egypt and back here tae Tobruk.

LAVERY	Incredible landscape. It's like being on a different planet.
MAC	Hae ya no been ta the desert afore, sir?
LAVERY	No McPhail.
MAC	Oh hell, yer in fer a treat.
LAVERY	It's exactly as I pictured it. No surprises so far.
MAC	Lucky you. Oh, sir, a few words a' advice, Captain. Oot here in the desert when the sun is right overheed and you've no shadow ya can feel like you're a mirage ... and it feels like you cou' put yer han' right through yer ain belly.
LAVERY	Really?
MAC	Oh aye ... but dinny try it. It's just a trick in yer mind.
LAVERY	Of course. Well thank you for the warning.
MAC	Ma pleasure ... oh ... and if you ever get the feeling that your legs are covered with small creepy crawlies ... it's cause they are ... sand mites. Wee buggers.
LAVERY	Good to know.
MAC	Oh yes. I had to figure that one out on ma own.

They arrive at the tent.

MAC	Here ya are. It's na exactly The Savoy ... but nicer than most.

MAC puts down LAVERY's bag inside.

MAC	There ya go, sir. Snug as a bug.
LAVERY	This will be fine. Yes. Thank you.
MAC	Nae skin aff my arse, sir. If ya need anthin' else jus gie us a holler.
LAVERY	McPhail?
MAC	Sir?
LAVERY	Isn't your tartan just for parade?
MAC	Oh ... quite right, sir. Since Malta fell supplies hae bin scarce. It's either this or no troosers, sir.
LAVERY	I see.
MAC	Truth be told if I'm cut down this is how I'd like ta go.
LAVERY	I see.
MAC	Sir ... gab is yer here ta help Donaldson with oor offending strategy. S'at true?
LAVERY	Yes. Mostly to observe really.
MAC	Well ... if you don't mind me sayin,' sir I was expecting a scabby auld dug. You can't be more than twenty.
	Uh sorry, sir.
LAVERY	It's alright, McPhail. I hear it all the time. I'm twenty-two.
MAC	Me as well. Well, sir ... if I might say ... I've got some strategic ideas a' ma own floating around in ma' heed.
LAVERY	Oh yes.

MAC	Yes, sir. I say we bring in three thousand pipers. Start them marching towards the German front ... full blast. They'd be back in Berlin before tea time.
LAVERY	Thank you, Private. I'll keep that in mind.
MAC	Use it if ya want, sir. I'll no say a word.
LAVERY	Thank you.
	It's nice to have a chat, McPhail. I haven't really talked to a soul other than General Donaldson since I arrived.
MAC	Oh yes ... and he can go on a bit. Oh I didn'y mean...
LAVERY	Oh no ... it's all right McPhail. You can speak freely.
MAC	Sometimes I think he has it in for me. I canny pass wind withoot his notice. This morning he had me doin' press ups in the sun fer o'er an hour because I said the grub tasted like camel shite.
LAVERY	Oh yes. I know. I saw you.
MAC	Aye. I tried to hide my face. I didn'y think it was the best first impression to make wi an officer.
LAVERY	Not to worry. You made one.
	It's just that all officers need a whipping boy, McPhail. My Uncle is no different.
MAC	Yer uncle?
LAVERY	Yes.
MAC	Ah hell. I'm done for.

LAVERY   Not to worry, McPhail. Our secret.

MAC   Thank you, sir.

                I'll let ya get settled. I'll let ya get settled
                in, sir. Get yer things sorted oot.

LAVERY   Yes.

                DAVID grabs for his duffel bag.

LAVERY   Oh, McPhail ... here.

MAC   What, sir?

LAVERY   It's some Brylcream. My mother insisted I
                take three. Here. Take one?

MAC   Oh well, sir ... I don't think I should...

LAVERY   Of course you should.

MAC   I don't think I'm goin' ta any fancy baws
                soon.

LAVERY   Keep it in your kit. To thank you for your
                help.

                *LAVERY hands him the jar. Their hands
                touch.*

MAC   Well ... this is the life. Most officers willny
                gie us the time of day. Thank you, sir.

LAVERY   I think it's dangerous to separate the
                men. We have to remember we're fighting
                for the same thing.

MAC   Oh yes, sir. The same thing. To gie hame.

LAVERY   Yes.

                Exactly.

To go home.

Thank you, Private.

MAC   Sir.

> *MAC salutes and leaves the tent. He
> opens the tube and smells it. He puts
> some on his hand and runs it through his
> hair. Aircraft noise overhead. The sound
> of world war two fighter aircraft.*
>
> *The lighting shifts. ESTHER enters,
> tucks in MAC's shirt puts a bow tie on
> him and combs the Brylcream through
> his hair.*
>
> *He is now TOM. The sound becomes the
> piercing sound of a modern jet.
> Andy Stewart singing 'A Scottish
> Soldier' can be heard playing on a record
> player.*

STEWART   (*on recording*)
                ...and now this soldier, this Scottish sol-
                dier, will wander far no more and soldier
                far no more
                And on a hillside, a Scottish hillside,
                you'll see a piper play his soldier home.
                He's seen the glory
                He's told the story
                Of battles glorious
                Of deeds victorious
                The bugles cease now
                He is at peace now
                Far from those green hills of Tyrole.
                Because those green hills are not
                Highland hills or the island hills, they're
                not my land's hills.
                And fair as these green foreign hills may
                be they are not the hills of home.

> *The lighting shifts to a small living room*

	in Scotland. TOM and ESTHER sit in silence as MARY, ESTHER's younger sister sings with the record and sobs.
MARY	(*singing with record*) ...because those green hills are not Highland hills or the island hills they're not my land's hills And fair as these green foreign hills may be they are not the hills of hooome.
	The song ends. Silence. *MARY pulls herself together.*
MARY	So yeas had a good flight then?
TOM	Yeah, Auntie Mary. Other than the nine hour delay.
ESTHER	We told you, Mary. It was a hellish journey with the great unwashed.
MARY	Oh right. Sorry, hen.
ESTHER	Damn charters. I really could have taken a life.
	Silence.
MARY	It was nice ta ha' ta drive a wee distance. Ta the airport. I'm just after getting my license.
TOM	You'd never know.
MARY	Only my third time on my own. No bad.
TOM	But I should tell ... you were on the wrong side the whole way.
MARY	Wha? O yes! Good Tom. It's aw backwards oer' there. I'm likin' the drivin'. It's the flying terrifies me. Doesny' make any

sense does it? All that metal just up in the air! Suspended like that! Gives me the heebie jeebies!! I just did it the once ... to Canada. Oh twice right ... I had ta get back!

Oh ya know, I have to thank you for our visit to Canada ... it was lovely.

ESTHER   Mary, that was fifteen years ago. You've thanked me quite enough.

MARY   Well it was lovely! Really fifteen years? Hell's bells. We went to that Ontario Place ... lovely ... and the zoo. It's so big that Canada ... too much space ... you could get lost.

TOM   Remember the water slide?

MARY   Oh aye, Tom. We gah aw wet.

ESTHER   It was a water slide.

MARY   I know.

Silence.

MARY   Wha' a fright I got.

Silence.

MARY   Esther? A wee bit more whiskey?

ESTHER   Oh no, I couldn't. Thank you, Mary. We don't drink as much in Canada.

MARY   Oh aye.

MARY pours herself another.

MARY   Smell you.

Another wee goldie fer you, Tom?

TOM   No thanks, Auntie Mary. I think I had one too many on the plane.

ESTHER   That man stewardess was pouring you doubles.

TOM   He's an old friend.

MARY   Oh hell. Up in the airieplane a' the time? What's his name?

TOM   Pride'95.

ESTHER   Tom.

TOM   Maybe just a splash more, Auntie Mary.

MARY   Aye. Fer Da.

She pours him a refill.

MARY   Oh it's bein' in the plane that's wha' it is ... it more than doubles it ... the alcohol ... the effect. When yer up in the air like that. I read that I did. Yer flyin' twice as high. Wheeeeee!

ESTHER   Mary, please. We're jet lagged.

MARY   Sorry, hen.

MARY   I rarely take a nip mesel'.

ESTHER   Oh? Making up for lost time?

TOM   We should drink. Tradition. It's a wake right?

TOM holds out his glass. She fills it.

TOM   Or is that more Irishey? What's the tradi-

	tion? Is there something we should slaughter?
ESTHER	We're not Vikings, Tom.
TOM	What?
	She pulls out some toffee from her purse.
ESTHER	Here, have some toffee.
TOM	No. Thank you ... Mum.
	TOM smiles at ESTHER.
MARY	I hope you'll be awright in Mac's room, Tom.
TOM	Yeah. Thanks. I... I didn't know you lived together.
MARY	Oh yes, Tom. I moved back here. Hame. It was perfect. There was no question. Our room was just the same, Esther. Well, you know yer uncle Frank vamoosed with a wee chickie?
TOM	No.
ESTHER	I forgot to mention it.
MARY	Best thing that ever hapn'd ta me ... snippy bugger.
	Silence.
ESTHER	The house's still the same then.
MARY	Oh no, Esther. We've painted ... new upholstery, bars on the windy. Oh yeah, and we've got the heat now.
ESTHER	Well the neighbuorhood's definitely not

what it use to be.

MARY   Oh no? What the hell is it then?

              Silence.

MARY   Oh ... it's say good ta see ya, Tom. So
              many years n' tears.

              I canny gei oer it. Gie us another hug.
              Come on ... yer na' ta' big fer a squeeze.

              They hug.

MARY   Just a wee lad when I saw you last. Now
              luk at ya ... aw Canadian.

TOM   I can't help myself.

MARY   Ya look like yer Granda, Tom. At the air-
              port I says sufferin duck there's a familiar
              face. Oh look at that. Now I can see yer
              Da' in ya. Oh now yer Mac again, now
              Callum ... Da' ... yer Da' ... Da' ... yer Da
              ... Da' ... yer Da'...

ESTHER   Mary! He can't look like Mac and Callum.

MARY   O'curse he can, Esther. It a' gies mixed in
              like a big stew. Mac's the tatties, Callum's
              the beef an' yer the carrots.

ESTHER   Why am I the carrots?

MARY   Ya just are.

TOM   Yup.

MARY   Ta Da' an' Callum.

              She raises her glass and takes a swig.

MARY   I'll warn ya son ... you'll take some rib-

bin' fer the kilt ... but if anyone says anything you give them what fer. More
power to ya. It's yer heritage. Just don't
say I know yeah.

MARY laughs at her own joke.

MARY   Oh, I'm just havin' ya on son. It's a braw sight.

ESTHER   Oh, Mary. I want Da' buried in it.

MARY   What?

ESTHER   His kilt. I want Da' buried in it. With his medals.

MARY   Oh no. But Esther, I ... he's

ESTHER   I don't want to argue about it, Mary.

MARY   Oh no, Esther ... I wasny...

ESTHER   It's my one request. We'll get to the parlour early.

MARY   Aye, hen. Righto.

She starts crying again.

ESTHER   Mary please.

MARY   Oh. I canny stop bubblin'. I canny believe it. I half expect him ta come in the room. "Mary? What's on the telly? I'm no watchin' nae soaps. Oh Esther ... I've got a picture of Mac for the service. He's all tan in the desert, in his tartan. He looks like a pop star.

ESTHER   He was a smart looking man.

MARY   He talked about you and your Mum aw

the time, Tom. Off in Canada. He was
thrilled for you. Oh Esther he was so
strong till the end. No' a day sick in his
life. He'd walk for miles each day. His
wee adventures he called them. He was a
good laugh Tom. We were chums.

MARY gets a refill.

ESTHER   I hope everything's taken care of for
tomorrow, Mary.

MARY   Aye, hen. I've bin on the blower a' day.
I got the wee chapel at St. Andrew's.
Early though. We've got ta get oot by
nine fer a double baptism

ESTHER   I would have preferred the cathedral.

MARY   Really? Wha' a surprise. There's a wed-
din'. Oh God I wonder if Frank'll show
his mug. Ay half wish he does soe ya kud
see his birdie, Tom.

TOM   Oh yeah?

MARY   A right ratbag she is too. No even four
feet tall. Diddies oot ta' here. She's a freak
really. Frank met her at the race track.
Her husband killed in a oil-rig explosion
... and she got a settlement ... 10,000
poun'. Nae bad, eh? So she takes a shine
to Frank. Now they live over the currie
and fish and chip. Lovely too! Big bay
windy. Since yer family, I can tell you
I've been havin' the most wonderful sex
with a Mr. Pokolopolous who runs the
motor shop. It's been a real perk.

TOM   Cheers! To Mr. Pokolopolous.

MARY   Hallelujah!

ESTHER	Mary! I don't remember asking.
MARY	Oh. Neither dae I, Esther.

MARY puts another record on. She sings and dances to Tom Jones' "It's Not Unusual". TOM joins in.

As the dance continues, MARY playfully puts her hand up TOM's kilt.
This is too much for ESTHER

ESTHER	Could you both please display a fragment of dignity!

MARY scratches the record off the turn table.

ESTHER	I'm sorry, Mary. It's been a long ... life.
MARY	It's a' right pet. A' are nerve's are ragged.
ESTHER	Yes. It's been lovely to catch up but we should all be unconscious.
MARY	Yes, Esther. We'll double up as usual.
ESTHER	Yes.
MARY	End of the hall, Tom.

It's just strange ... with Da' gone now.

They all exit. A lighting shift time passage.
Later that night. TOM re-enters. He checks to see if he is alone then lights a cigarette. He is alone for a few drags. Then MARY appears and whispers.

MARY	Ah ha. I knew it!. Caught ya?
TOM	Did I wake you, Auntie Mary?

MARY   Shhhhhh! Oh no, pet. I cou' sleep through a nuclear meltdown.

TOM   Is it alright if I...?

MARY   Oh aye son. Yer Granda smoked a pack a' unfiltered a day. I miss it aready. Gie us a drag.

               MARY takes a drag.

MARY   Ahhhh. My first in six mnoths. Lovely. A wee rush.

               Ohhhhh. Can ya no sleep, luv?

TOM   No.

MARY   Aye. Yer clock's a'will nilly. Yer Mum's sawi'n wood.

               Da ya think she's aright, Tom?

TOM   Uh ... no.

MARY   No.

               They both burst out laughing.

MARY   Shhhhh!

               Oh, son. I luv yer Mum, I dae. We was right close when we were wee. I'd help her before her competitions. Make sure her gear was no fankled. Are ya no still dancin, Tom?

TOM   Sometimes.

MARY   Any meadals?

TOM   Some honourable mentions. I dance at a bar ... a pub.

ESTHER comes into the edge of light.

MARY   Oh, show business! Yer cousin Kylie was in a band fer a wee while. Away's aff rehearsin' here an there with her wee punky pals. If that lead singer had had both her ears they coulda gone top o' the pops.

TOM   I'll see her tomorrow at the service.

MARY   Oh no, luv. My poor wee girl. She's still in the clink. She's like Frank. She's got a temper. They've a weight room though. She looks lovely.

ESTHER enters the scene.

MARY   Oh Esther. Sorry, hen. Did we wake ya?

ESTHER   Yes.

MARY   Me an' the lad was just hain' a wee pow woo.

ESTHER   And an addictive substance.

TOM   You told me Kylie was in art school

ESTHER   What? Oh ... I'm sure they've got arts and crafts.

MARY   Aye. She made me a mithers day card.

ESTHER   Ya see? Happy ending. Now lets all get to bed.

MARY   Ya know ... I've never seen ya dance, Tom. Yer Mum sent snaps though.

TOM   I'll give you a fling later.

ESTHER   Over my dead body.

MARY Oh. That would be a treat.

TOM Why didn't you dance, Auntie Mary?

MARY Oh no, darlin'. I'm no fussy for it. But me and the accordion are still very good friends.

ESTHER Yes.

TOM What was my dad like, Auntie Mary?

ESTHER Tom. It's late.

TOM What? I'm climbing up the family tree. That's why we're here isn't it?

MARY Aye. Oh Tom we're a twisted lot. Mac an' me were dain' a family tree thingme ... looking up aw' the genealogy an that'. Nuthin' but a bunch of nutters top ta bottom. Oh ... other than the Duchess here of course.

ESTHER Mary.

MARY Oh I'm sorry, luv, but sometimes you'd think yer shite didny smell.

TOM I don't think she does that, Aunty Mary. It's number one all the way.

ESTHER Dear God

MARY Ya know I went ta the picture wi Callum a few times afore yer ma' got her claws inta im. Eh, Esther?

ESTHER You're having hallucinations.

MARY Ah Esther, me an' Callum were peas in a' pod.

ESTHER	I don't remember.
MARY	Oh aye. Memory loss.
ESTHER	Let's not go into ancient history. Mary. I've had enough for one day. My Da's deed.
MARY	Yes. I know he's deed, Esther. I found him. Sittin' right there a book on his lap, a smile on his face. Yes, Esther I know.
TOM	Have you got a picture of Callum?
MARY	You've no seen a picture of yer Da, Tom?
ESTHER	I packed light. You've seen the caricature he had done at Hadley Fair
TOM	So he had a really big head and a really small body and always had a soccer ball spinning on his head?
MARY	No far off. Oh Tom ... they've got a brilliant picture of yer Da' up at the pub. The Crown an' Rabbit. The snap that was in the paper! They still talk about that game!
TOM	What game?
MARY	The World Cup son.
ESTHER	Mary!
MARY	Wha'?
ESTHER	Don't.
MARY	Does the lad na know, Esther?
TOM	What?

MARY   I shoulda' bloody known.Yer father died a hero, Tom. A national hero.

ESTHER He was a local arse!

TOM   What? Tell me.

MARY   Get started or I will, Esther. Callum deserved that.

ESTHER Oh bloody hell! Stupid fitba' game. That's what it was. It was the world cup. So, of course, they were all pissed. And then the Portuguese team won the game. And because they won the game, your father and half of Glasgow were going to kill the Portuguese players! They were going to cut their throats with broken beer bottles! He climbed a barbed wire fence, fell broke his neck then was trampled to death.

        There. Are you happy?

        Stunned silence.

TOM   I... I...

MARY   He was the first one at the fence. Fist in the air "May you drown in your own blood! That's the picture they got for the paper.

        Silence.

TOM   Trampled?

ESTHER Oh don't romanticize him, Mary.

TOM   How could you even consider not telling me that? You said he died in a car accident. You said that he was this quiet little bookish guy with faulty brakes. Have you lost your mind?

ESTHER   I remember they tried to fill the cleat marks on his face with putty. Did you need to know that?

TOM   Yes!

ESTHER   That's enough of that. It's only Mac's death that brings us back here now.

MARY   Aye. Maybe you'll come back for mine.

ESTHER   We'll see.

TOM   Was he even a teacher?

MARY   Sometimes he cleaned floors at the skul.

TOM   Fuck!

ESTHER   Language.

TOM   You are ... you are truly a piece of work. Oh yeah, by the way ... that picture you have at home. Of the house where you were supposedly brought up? It looks nothing like this house. Okay? It is not this house. THIS IS AN APARTMENT!

ESTHER   Well, do you think they'd put this on a postcard?

TOM   It's all bullshit!

MARY   You can't be too hard on yer wee Mum, Tom. She just likes ta take out the bad bits.

TOM   Yeah. And we're all the shitty little bad bits eh, Mum?

You know. I was trying very hard to be

	sweet! I was. I think I was doing pretty good too. But you make it very difficult!
ESTHER	So I tidied things up a little. So that's what happened to your Dad. Mindless thug. I guess that explains some things. Of course I often wonder now, maybe with his influence you wouldn't be ... uh .. quite so...
TOM	What?
ESTHER	Well you know ... you might be more...
MARY	What, Esther?
TOM	Say it.
ESTHER	MANLY!
TOM	That must be it. Yeah. If only I'd had hooliganism!
MARY	Oh ... you're a wee bit bent then, eh?
TOM	Very much so, yes.
MARY	I had an inkling. Oh! I'll have ta mark that down on the tree.
ESTHER	Mary! Ah yes, tell the whole world. Esther McPhail's back with her koochy koo dancin' son. Let me tell you bodies are spinning, somewhere.
TOM	Oh just cut the Miss Jean Brodie shit for once please!
ESTHER	Shhhhh! Here. Have some toffee.
TOM	I don't want any toffee! You eat the fucking toffee! Choke on it!

ESTHER   How dare you!

TOM   You have a serious toffee problem!

ESTHER   Control yourself.

TOM   No. I am the son of Callum Robertson, hoodlum hero. I'll do what I want. And Mac? A war hero? He was probably just some fuckin' broken down crazy drunk at the local pub?

ESTHER slaps him.

MARY   Yer Granda got the Desert Star son. That part's true.

TOM starts to leave.

ESTHER   Where are you going?

TOM   Up a tree. For a walk. I don't know.

ESTHER   Don't be an idiot. You'll get lost.

TOM   I enjoy getting lost, Mrs. Robertson. It's one of my most favourite things to do.

ESTHER   I'm coming with you. I will not have you roaming the streets to all hours.

TOM   I don't think so sweetie! FORGET ABOUT IT! SIT! NO! You are not coming with me! No. You are staying her.

MARY   Oh hell! What have I done?

TOM   No. It wasn't you.

ESTHER   You listen and listen good Thomas Robertson! If you miss the service tomorrow I will track you down like a dog and break your legs. Bright and early!

TOM exits.

Silence.

ESTHER   Oh hell!

She yells at him.

ESTHER   BRING BACK THAT KILT!

He is long gone.

ESTHER   Bloody hell. I just want to get this over with and get back home.

MARY   Oh ... but you are home, Esther.

Lights out on MARY and ESTHER.

The lighting shifts outside. TOM yells to the sky on the street in Glasgow .

TOM   MAY YOU DROWN IN YOUR OWN BLOOD!

We hear far off rumbling of a shell exploding. The lighting shifts back to the desert. TOM is now MAC. He yells under his breath.

MAC   May ya drown in yer own blood! Bloody kraut bastards!! Can ya no keep it doon?

He hears something in the dark and he senses someone there.

MAC   Hallo?

Silence.

MAC   Whose there? Ollie ollie oxen free.

LAVERY emerges from the dark.

MAC   Oh Captain Lavery. Ya enjoyin yer first
                    night here sir?

LAVERY   It's quite the experience.

MAC   You should be in side, sir.

LAVERY   No. I came out for the shelling.

MAC   Sir?

LAVERY   I wanted to experience it first hand. I
                    imagine they're just reminding us they're
                    still there.

MAC   I never forget.

LAVERY   We are completely safe. Intelligence is not
                    anticipating any advancement for some-
                    time. And they're too far out of range to
                    do any damage.

MAC   They tend ta surprise ya, sir.

LAVERY   It's a thinly veiled attempt to provoke us.
                    To unsettle us.

                    A shell explodes a closer distance away.
                    LAVERY swallows hard.

LAVERY   Dear God.

                    LAVERY starts to hyperventilate.

MAC   You a'right, sir?

LAVERY   What? Oh yes. Yes. Just getting my legs
                    so to speak.

MAC   Oh aye. Where was ya stationed last, sir?

LAVERY   HQ Dover.

MAC   Wha'

LAVERY   This is my first time at the front, Private.

MAC   Oh? Well ... .you've picked a right dilly,
             sir.

LAVERY   Yes actually, I did.

MAC   Ya really picked it, sir?

LAVERY   Yes. My father suggested Tobruk. I
             agreed. I wanted to get out from behind
             the desk for a while. I wanted to be right
             in the heart of it not staring at a map.

             *Another shell explodes in the closer dis-
             tance. DAVID heaves more heavily*

LAVERY   Holy Mary Mother of God!

MAC   I didny' know you were a Tim, sir.

LAVERY   What ... oh yes. I'll be crossing myself in a
             minute,

MAC   Bloody hell, lad. Wha' are ya gonna be
             like when they're no three miles away?

LAVERY   I don't know.

MAC   When yer tickets cawed in there's no a
             thing ya can Da. You jus' ha' ta live yer
             life. I awas feel like I'm on borrowed
             time. I jus canny believe we're no doin'
             anythin' They've got us all surrounded ...
             we should bash back.

LAVERY   We have to wait 'til the appropriate time.

MAC   Tell me, sir, what is it ya dae exactly. Na
             offense. What is a strategy a' war?

LAVERY	Well. It's hard to condense... It's always being one step ahead of your opponent. You have to think like them. Put yourselves in their shoes ... and therefore be able to anticipate every move. Even implement actions that will cause the enemy to react in a desired way.
MAC	Complicated.
LAVERY	Common sense mostly.

Another explosion closer. LAVERY heaves and pulls in tight to MAC.

LAVERY	Maybe I'm not really built for this.
MAC	Naebody is, sir. It's nae natural ... I'll gie ya that much ... but ya dae get used ta It's nae sae bad in the daylight.
LAVERY	Yes. You're right. Today I was staring into the horizon and the sand of desert and the sky seemed to melt into a single colour. I completely lost my balance. Is that to be expected?
MAC	Oh yes, sir. Quite common, sir. An' the land changes a' the time. Everyday ya wake up in a whole new battlefield.

Another explosion.

MAC	It's jus' the bogeyman sir.
LAVERY	Private?
MAC	The boogeyman sir. When I was a lad an' I was afeard of the bogeyman my Mum would rock me in her arms and say ... now now now ... yer my wee man ... remember that ... nothin can hurt ya now.

Older LAVERY (DAVID) enters carrying a small suitcase and sees the two men. He watches them from a distance. CAPTAIN LAVERY crosses to older DAVID and exits past him.

A lighting shift to present day Scotland at night. The sound of traffic horns, a train rumbling in the distance. DAVID is now watching TOM in George Square, Glasgow. He crosses in front of TOM, stops and looks back. Their eyes meet.

TOM sits up. DAVID heads away then turns to look at TOM. He stands close to TOM. TOM notices him staring. After a while TOM gets annoyed.

TOM   Hello.

DAVID   What? Oh ... yes ... hello.

TOM   You ... uh ... want something?

DAVID   Excuse me, lad?

TOM   You were staring at me.

DAVID   Oh, I apologize. Was I?

TOM   Yeah.

DAVID   Oh. Well. I thought... No.

    I'm sorry. My train was late ... and I was heading through the square ... to ... my hotel ... and...

TOM   Yeah ... look ... I'm not from here... I mean if you're looking for directions or anything ... okay? Bye-bye.

DAVID   No. I know my way around. I'm just ...

well, I don't know.

I saw you there and ... I...

Do you mind if I join you?

TOM   Yeah. I do. I... I'm not doing anything.

DAVID   No? It seemed to me like you were look-
             ing at the stars.

TOM   No.

DAVID   They're very useful. They're the only way
             we really know where we are. The prox-
             imity ... the relationship to ... uh well ...
             there ... you see? That's Mars ... it's a little
             pink. And Orion to the left.

             Are you interested in astronomy?

TOM   No. Could you please ... ya know ... fuck-
             off?

DAVID   Oh, you're an American.

TOM   Canadian! Man ... .what is it with ... this
             country? Nothing but a bunch natterers!
             Nattering on about nothing.

DAVID   I see this is a bad time for a chat.

TOM   Yes.

DAVID   That's a shame.

TOM   Look ... it's your country. Do what ever
             you want with it.

DAVID   Why, thank you.

             Silence. DAVID takes in a deep breath.

DAVID   It's a grand night.

                 Silence. He looks at TOM.

DAVID   Glasgow's got an energy all it's own.

                 Silence.

DAVID   Tell me, what is it you do back in
                 Canada?

TOM   Are you still here?

DAVID   I'm afraid so, lad.

TOM   Do you always talk to strangers in the
                 middle of the night?

DAVID   I try not to make it a habit.

TOM   I bet.

DAVID   I taught there for a year once. Canada.
                 Montreal.

TOM   English?

DAVID   What? Oh no. Military History. That's my
                 field. You?

                 Silence.

TOM   I'm an exotic performer.

DAVID   In Canada? Well, what do you know? In a
                 circus?

TOM   Yeah. Sort of.

DAVID   That's interesting.

TOM   It has it's moments.

DAVID	Did you have a chance to travel around while you were here?
TOM	No. I've been walking around for a couple of hours. Does that count? Plus the airport. A small living room ... and this uh ... square.
DAVID	That's a shame. I'm David.
TOM	Tartan Tom.
DAVID	Delightful.

Silence.

DAVID	That's a lovely kilt. There was a time you wouldn't see one anywhere. Now they've become a bit fashionable.
	Lovely.
TOM	I am a victim of fashion.
DAVID	Good strong legs.
TOM	Pardon?
DAVID	You've got a dancer's legs.

Silence.

DAVID	I've a grand idea Mr. Tartan. Why don't you join me for wee drink.
TOM	You're a sly one aren't you.
DAVID	Sorry?
TOM	Look ... thanks, that's very Scottish of you and everything ... but I'm busy ... you know, looking at the stars and everything...

DAVID   I see.

TOM   Misunderstanding. I didn't know... I did-
             n't know this was the cruising ... type
             area or whatever...

DAVID   Oh no, lad, no. That's Blytheswood
             Square.

TOM   Oh. So you're not trying to pick me up?

DAVID   Oh my. No, lad! I don't think so. Is that a
             possibility?

TOM   No.

DAVID   Right. Well ... I hadn't really thought
             about it. Oh I see. No, no, no lad. Another
             day maybe.

             You were quite a picture lounging there.
             That's all really.

TOM   I thought maybe you were trying to...

DAVID   Not to worry, lad. I'll take it as a compli-
             ment.

             There's also a pub ... if that's what you're
             looking for, The Bull's Head ... two streets
             down.

TOM   No. No. Thanks. Is that where you're
             headed?

DAVID   No. It's getting a little late. I'll just head
             to the hotel. Nice nattering with you
             Tom. I was feeling a bit off tonight and
             you've set me right.

             He turns and comes right back.

DAVID   I'm going to be forward again and ask

you to join me for a bite back at my hotel.

TOM   You don't give up do you?

DAVID No, lad. I guess not.

TOM   You know it's ... well ... bad timing... I've recently become celibate.

DAVID Well, well ... what a lucky coincidence.

TOM thinks for a moment.

TOM   Room service?

DAVID Oh yes. Anything you want.

TOM   Far?

DAVID The Copthorne. Right across the street.

TOM   Celibate.

DAVID Yes. I won't forget.

They head off.

DAVID Do you have a show tomorrow?

TOM   Oh yes. Bright and early.

DAVID and TOM exit..

Act Two

In the blackness we hear an announcer.

MC   Ladies and gentlemen our last finalist in the ladies seventeen and under representing Clydebank — Esther McPhail.

ESTHER walks into a half light. She assumes the starting stance for a fling. The pipes begin playing. Bagpipes start and she prepares to dance. She goes up on her toes.

MARY sits up in bed.

MARY   Esther?

The lights shift back to a bedroom at the house in Glasgow, present day. The bagpipes drone to silence. They are both in pyjamas. ESTHER grabs her foot in pain.

ESTHER   Jesus, Mary!

MARY   Oh sorry, luv.

ESTHER   You've given me a heart attack!

MARY   Sorry pet. Were ya dancin', Esther?

ESTHER   Don't be ridiculous, Mary.

MARY	Of course not.
MARY	It's past two, luv. You shou' gae back ta sleep.
ESTHER	I can't sleep, Mary. My head's spinning.
MARY	Oh... I'm sure he's fine. Just off exploring.
ESTHER	You have no idea, Mary.
MARY	No.
ESTHER	Besides, Mary. I'm on the wrong side of the room. That used to be my side.
MARY	Oh aye. That's right. It was.

MARY lays back down.

MARY	I'll catch up on ma' Jackie Collins. I can tell it's building up ta a dirty bit.

MARY reads for a while.

MARY	Ah right. Here it is. "Cassandra caressed his pulsating python of love..." Well, bully fer Cassandra ....
ESTHER	Mary, please. I don't want to have dreams.
MARY	Right. Oh crimmy! Looka at tha'.
ESTHER	No more, Mary.
MARY	No. My book mark! I forgot. I found a picture a' Callum fer Tom.

She reveals a small black and white snapshot.

MARY	When he took me ta' the Barrowland

Ballroom. Oh... I'm in it as well. But we can always rip that part oot.

ESTHER   Don't do that, Mary. I've got scissors in my purse.

MARY   Aye. A long time ago. And look what ya got. He's a braw lad, Esther. Full of sparks.

ESTHER   Yes.

MARY   Yes, Esther.

Silence.

ESTHER   I hope you've ordered the flowers for tomorrow. People always forget about the flowers.

MARY   Oh uh ... yes, hen. Two lovely vases.

ESTHER   And overflowing with roses for Mum?

MARY   Oh yes, Esther. Roses for Rose. Red roses. But Esther the vases are no very big. They just sit either side of the ... urn.

ESTHER   Urn? What urn? Urn? They cremated him?

MARY   Yes, Esther.

ESTHER   What?

MARY   I should have told you earlier. But you were so intent on his kilt . So.... I...

ESTHER   I don't believe this! Burned up? Yer a right idjit sometimes, Mary McPhail! How could you do that?

MARY   It was Dad's request, Esther!

ESTHER	He never told me that.
MARY	He told me, Esther! Three years ago. We talked about it all the time. "I dinny want to be planted" ... he said ..."dust ta dust". Burned as soon as possible. Only an urn at the service.
ESTHER	I really would liked to have at least seen him.
MARY	It's too bad you didn't see him more when he was movin'!

Silence.

MARY	Oh Esther, he looked great. I had to pick out the suit and all that and well they'd got him all painted up. I combed his hair It was a' shiny and lovely. I put that wee twist at the front like he used to do when he'd come to the Pub on Sundays. All that just to burn him up. Strange, uh?
ESTHER	I sent him the air tickets. He wouldn't come.
MARY	I know, hen. He liked ta stay close ta home. He was away's hopin' you'd come back ta see him.
ESTHER	I tried, Mary. A few times. I just couldn't get on the plane alone.
MARY	Look at us, eh Esther? Two old birds, eh? Who'd uh thought? Oh Esther, we're orphans.
ESTHER	Yes, Mary.
MARY	Auld orphans.
	First Mum. I kilt her, remember? My big

fat heed. Split her open. We only had an hour together but I swear I can remember her.

My second earliest memory is of you callin' me a murderer.

ESTHER   It was a wee joke between sisters, Mary.

MARY   Oh yes. Very funny.

Silence.

ESTHER   Was he awright, Mary? Da?

MARY   Oh aye, pet. I'll no tell a lie. He wasny aw' there fer a wee while. But aways a joke. He'd still tak oot yer dancin' medals sometimes.

ESTHER   Burned up. It's no right. It's no right.

Lights cross to TOM and DAVID in the hotel room. Sitting apart. TOM is finishing a plate of blood pudding.

DAVID   How was your blood pudding?

TOM   Uh ... perfectly disgusting.

DAVID   Is that good?

TOM   Oh yeah. Did you want some?

DAVID   No lad, thanks.

TOM   I had a craving.

DAVID   Oh?

TOM   Yeah. My mother got me hooked when I was a baby. I've gone clean for periods of time ... but it always pulls me back in.

DAVID   Oh. How sad. Sometimes I can't get
               enough chocolate. It's one of my weak-
               nesses.

TOM   That and nice legs.

DAVID   I'm guilty there.

DAVID   So you're not sorry you came?

TOM   No. Should I be?

DAVID   No, no.

TOM   You seem pretty harmless.

DAVID   Thank you. I suppose that's meant as a
               compliment.

TOM   Yeah.

DAVID   I feel a trifle guilty about dragging you
               away from your meditations.

TOM   No. I was just ... you know getting lost.
               Walking for a couple of hours. Looking
               for the Crown and Rabbit.

DAVID   Don't know that one. A friend used to
               take me to the Randall Room. Too much
               velvet.

TOM   Where did the train come from?

DAVID   Edinburgh, lad. I'm here until tomorrow.

TOM   Married?

DAVID   Oh, you want my particulars. I see. No,
               no. I never married. Almost once. An
               unfortunate-looking girl from Dundee.

TOM   Hmm? I had you pegged as a married

	weekender. You know ... down in the city for some slap and tickle. I can usually spot them. Where I work ... they make up some of the clientele.
DAVID	Oh yeah? Wringling Brothers'?
TOM	Yeah. When I'm in the centre ring surveying the public. You can suss them out pretty quick.
DAVID	I see. Do you balance things?
TOM	I've been known to. I'm quitting soon. Show business ain't all it's cracked up to be.

Silence.

TOM	Well ... you know ... I gotta get going. Thanks for the pudding.
DAVID	Eat and run?
TOM	Well ... I do kinda feel like you're expecting something and I...
DAVID	My ... you have a healthy view of yourself, don't you? Please believe me. I'm just enjoying the company.
TOM	Hey ... you could hurt a guy's feelings. Not your type?
DAVID	To a tee. You are very beautiful. And celibate.
TOM	Yeah.
DAVID	How long have you been celibate?
TOM	Almost forty-eight hours.

DAVID   Oh. How's it going so far?

TOM   So far so good. I decided yesterday. After work.

DAVID   So you don't have a pal back home?

TOM   A pal? Oh a pal. No. I did a while ago but I don't anymore.

DAVID   That's a shame.

TOM   Is it? I guess.

Silence.

TOM   The truth is, David ... I'm a table dancer.

DAVID   Oh?

TOM   Yeah. It's where you dance on a ... table...

DAVID   Yes. I'm familiar with the concept.

TOM   Right. So ... yeah, anyway ... I get lots of opportunities to ... get dates, you know? Meet people ... from my pedestal. It's a job bonus.

DAVID   Oh, an adventurer.

TOM   Yeah. I like the way you put that. I was. Yeah. But I've had enough. I'm tired of the nasty entanglements of the flesh.

DAVID   Then you're probably doing it wrong.

TOM   Oh yeah?

DAVID   Yes. How was it forty-eight hours ago?

TOM   Faceless.

DAVID   Well, not everything can be a romance.

TOM   Yeah. I would describe it as ... goal orient-
               ed.

DAVID   A race to the finish? I've had lovers like
               that. Very frustrating. Why would any-
               one want to get it over with?

TOM   I just do.

DAVID   Oh.

TOM   Do ... you still ... uh?

DAVID   When the winds blowing the right way. It
               takes a little longer ... but I don't
               begrudge the time.

TOM   You know you're very funny for some-
               one...

DAVID   This old?

TOM   I didn't mean it like that.

DAVID   Yes you did.

TOM   Yeah ... I did. Do you? Have a pal?

DAVID   Not at the moment.

TOM   Ever?

DAVID   Yes. Mitchell and I were together for
               twelve years. He had a bypass and he
               was doing fine but I lost him three years
               ago. And Taylor before that. Twenty-three
               years. Motorcycle accident. Daft bugger.

TOM   It must have been hard to meet anyone
               back then.

DAVID   Don't kid yourself, lad. Did you think
            you'd invented it? It was just a different
            world. We were confirmed bachelors ...
            travelling companions.

TOM   Strange sisters.

DAVID   Yes. I guess you have it easier now. I
            don't know. But then, there was always
            someone's eye to catch if you were look-
            ing. Why do you think people look on the
            war so fondly?

            It turned everything upside down and
            everyone looked the other way.
            Distracted. You met people you would
            have never met. You were thrown togeth-
            er. You had no future ... you had no past.
            Everything was possible.

            Silence.

DAVID   Tom?

TOM   Yeah?

DAVID   Tom, why are you here? In Glasgow?

TOM   Family, I guess.

DAVID   Oh?

TOM   Yeah. A funeral. My Grandfather.

DAVID   Yes. Of course. I'm so very sorry.

TOM   I never met him.

DAVID   What a shame.

            Silence.

DAVID   Tom. I was wondering if I might...?

	I would very much like to hold you.
TOM	I don't think...
DAVID	Just hold you. That's all. You can run faster than me.

Silence.

TOM lies across DAVID's lap. DAVID puts his arms around him.

DAVID	Is that all right?
TOM	Yes.
DAVID	What happened with your friend back home.
TOM	Marco?
DAVID	Marco.
TOM	Yeah. I don't know. He, he... Marco. So beautiful.
DAVID	Yes?
TOM	Yes. And warm. Down to his bones. Sticky. Beautiful. Marco. You really want to know?
DAVID	Yes.
TOM	Almost a year. Pretty good. We met at the club. He was the new dancer. First time he saw me he said, "Your a dress is a very sesse".

He thought I was exotic in my tartan.

It's good to have a gimmick. He did a squeegee thing ... he would shine himself. |

It was kinda' vulgar ... but he made it work.

He moved in the next day. And then? I don't know. A year — then what? Every day for the rest of your life? I freaked, I guess. I started to think about us in thirty years. It just stretched out in front of me. I projected myself forward and back through time.

Terrifying. Where did it end? But it did. He left. He had to. Short and sweet. You know what I mean?

DAVID   Yes, I do. Short and sweet. North Africa, 1942.

TOM   Yeah?

DAVID   Yes. It was a magical place, Tom. I remember the darkness. On nights the shelling would stop, you could stretch out your arm and it would truly disappear. I fell in love in that darkness.

TOM   Yeah?

DAVID   A sweet ... kilted lad from Glasgow.

TOM   You fell in love with him?

DAVID   I don't know if I would have said it at the time. But looking back there's no question. He took my breath away. From the first moment I saw him. Pressing his chest into the earth. In his kilt. Years blur together in my mind but I can remember every second of every moment of that month we were together.

TOM   What happened to him? Was he killed?

DAVID   No. He made it home. He's being buried tomorrow.

TOM looks to DAVID. DAVID really looks at him then touches his face.

DAVID   You're his spitting image.

Silence.

TOM   So I've heard.

Silence.

TOM   Did he fall in love with you?

DAVID   I like to think so.

TOM   Wh ... when did you last see him?

DAVID   1957. I'd written him a letter saying I'd like to see him. He wrote back. A first. He stayed with me here at the Copthorne Hotel. We laughed, we sang some old songs. We held each other ... all night.

Silence.

DAVID   Do you mind me telling you?

TOM   No.

DAVID   I didn't think.

Silence.

DAVID   Tom?

TOM   Yeah.

DAVID   You're welcome to stay.

Mary and ESTHER enter singing a

Scottish hymn and they establish the
chapel. MARY is carrying the urn with a
huge purse, and ESTHER, an ornately
framed photo of MAC in the desert.

ESTHER
& MARY   Bonnie Charlie's gone awa'
Safely o'er the friendly main
Many a heart will break in twa'
Should he ne'r come back again
Will ye no come back again?
Will ye no come back again?
Better loved ya canna be.
Will ye no come back again?
"WILL YE NO COME BACK AGAIN?"

While they sing TOM and DAVID enter
and stand in behind them. ESTHER
glares at them. They sing along. The song
concludes.

TOM   Mum?

ESTHER   Don't you call me that!

ESTHER goes to exit.

TOM   Wait.

ESTHER   Wait? For you? I don't think so Buster
Brown. I did all night. And then late for
the service!

TOM   You're lucky I'm here at all!

ESTHER   Oh yes, very lucky. Hell, I've won the
sweepstakes! You could have been bludg-
eoned for all I knew. Yer Grandad's
funeral and you can't break your habits
for two days. I was humiliated!

TOM   I made it. I wanted to be here.

ESTHER   You're a disgrace.

MARY   Esther, don't get yer knickers in a twist.
                He's here the now. Are ya arigh' son?

TOM   Yes, Auntie Mary

ESTHER   The whole service was a disgrace. You,
                ten bar cronies, six sour-faced cousins ...
                one in track pants. And the only military
                representation an asthmatic piper.

MARY   He did no bad. He's only got the one
                lung.

                        ESTHER looks at DAVID.

ESTHER   Oh, here's one. Hello we're the begrieved.
                Did you come all on your lonesome
                General?

DAVID   Yes, but not to worry. I've got my name
                pinned to the inside of my jacket.

ESTHER   Yes. Better safe than sorry.

DAVID   That's my knee.

ESTHER   I'm sorry? In that photo of Mac in the
                desert. Beside him. That's my knee.

MARY   Oh what a braw knee ya had.

DAVID   Why, thank you.

TOM   (*re: the photo*) That's Mac?

DAVID   Like looking in mirror, isn't it?

ESTHER   Thank you for the medals, Corporal. Bye
                now.

TOM   This is David.

ESTHER   What?

TOM   David Lavery ... these are Mac's children.
            My Auntie Mary ... .and my mother,
            Esther.

DAVID   Good to see you.

TOM   I met David last night.

ESTHER   What? Last night? Last night?

TOM   Yeah. I was out walking around.

DAVID   Small world.

TOM   He gave me directions.

ESTHER   Oh. I see. Is that what they're calling it?

TOM   Don't.

MARY   Oh ... you must be Dad's wee pen pal?

DAVID   Yes. That's right, Mary.

MARY   Always scribblin' notes ta each other
            about the war.

DAVID   Yes. On and off for a number of years.

MARY   Esther, you remember Mr. Lavery? The
            Copthorne Hotel. Big juicy steaks.

TOM   You've already met?

ESTHER   Mr. Lavery?

DAVID   Yes, Esther. It's good to see you again. It's
            been a long time.

ESTHER   Let's scramble, Mary. We've got a plane
            to catch.

DAVID   Leaving so soon, Esther?

ESTHER   Yes. I find it much more interesting to be
               Scottish in Canada. People still look on it
               mistily. Come on, Mary. Shake a leg.

MARY   No.

ESTHER   What do you mean? No?

MARY   I mean no, Esther. I'm nae goin'. You
               head back. Just close the door behind ya.
               I'm sorry Tom but you'll hae ta get a taxi
               ta the arieplane. I'm no finished yet.

ESTHER   What are you on about?

MARY   Mac. It was his last wish. Ta be sprinkled
               alang the banks of the Clyde. To "catch
               the wind south" he said.

ESTHER   What colour's your sky, Mary?

MARY   You're welcome ta join me.

ESTHER   Are you making this up as you go along?
               You can just keep him on the mantel.

MARY   No. I'm goin'.

TOM   I'll go with you, Auntie Mary.

MARY   Oh ... that would be lovely, Tom.

DAVID   May I?

TOM   Yes, David. Of course.

ESTHER   There's nothing ta join. The service is
               over! You need a permit!

               ESTHER lunges at MARY.

ESTHER   Mary just give me that urn and get out
            the way!

MARY   Out of the way? That's nice. Esther,
            you're cruisin' for a brusin'! I'll tell you
            that much for free. It was his wish!
            You've got no say in the matter. You come
            floating in from Canada like the queen of
            bloody Sheba ... and you expect us all to
            act like we're the royal fookin family of
            Glasgow.

            Sorry, Mr. Lavery.

DAVID   As you were.

MARY   Yer Da' sold fish. From a cart. Esther? He
            named you Esther after Esther Williams.
            He thought you looked like a wee fish!

ESTHER   You don' know what yer talkin' abou'!

MARY   Oh don't I, Essie?? Maybe my memory's
            goin' too! What do you remember,
            Esther? DO YOU REMEMBER ME AT
            ALL? HALLO! I'M MARY! I'M YOUR
            SISTER!

ESTHER   Shut yer cake hole, Mary McPhail!

MARY   Aye. There's the Esther I remember. Yer
            Mum used ta be a right toughy, Tom. Yer
            just here crossing everyone off some list
            in yer mind ... "that one's deed that one's
            deed". Well I'm not deed, Esther!

ESTHER   It's like you're trying to make me crack.
            I'm only human for God's sake! I can
            only take so much. My Da's dead ... my
            sisters gone crackers ... my son is on the
            verge of becoming a high-class ... male
            prostitute ... serial killer...

TOM   What the hell are you talking about?

ESTHER   If you keep on the way you're going ...
                   that's where you're headed.

MARY   Don't be so hard on the lad, Esther!

ESTHER   I am not hard on him! I think I've been
                   remarkably accommodating!

TOM   Yes ... thank you for tolerating me.

ESTHER   I just feel sorry for you.

DAVID   Let's all try to calm down.

ESTHER   Yes, well thank you for that, skipper. But
                   the service is over. Maybe you should run
                   along before you hurt yourself.

TOM   Don't!

DAVID   You've got your Dad's spirit, Esther
                   McPhail.

ESTHER   How dare you.

DAVID   Tom, maybe it's best if I'm on my way.

TOM   No.

                   TOM turns to ESTHER

TOM   David is here for Mac. So am I! You?

ESTHER   This is not about me.

TOM   No it's not! We should get going.

MARY   Yes. The rain's broken. Ya comin,' Esther?

                   No repsonse.

DAVID	You should come, Esther. The walk will do you good.

ESTHER grabs the photo from TOM.

MARY	Right. Gentlemen.
TOM	You lead the way, Auntie Mary
MARY	Sorry about my outburst Mr. David. My nerves are ragged.
DAVID	Quite all right.

They exit leaving ESTHER and TOM.

The lighting shifts slightly to the desert. Is TOM now MAC? ESTHER thinks she may be seeing a ghost.

CAPTAIN LAVERY enters. ESTHER exits in the opposite direction. The lighting shifts completely to the desert.

LAVERY	McPhail!
MAC	Sir.
LAVERY	I need to have a word.
MAC	But of course, sir.
LAVERY	Yes, thank you, Private.

They travel a distance. They whisper. And maintain a military stance.

MAC	What is it, David?
LAVERY	Mac. Tonight. I...
MAC	Yer no standin' me up, are ya?

LAVERY   No. Well, yes. Mac. Word came through last night in the Officers' mess. At the celebration. One of Rommel's Panzer units has broken through the wires at the farthest perimeter at Gazala. They may be able to cross the tank ditches tonight with the Italians in tow.

MAC   Oh you've got ta be jokin.

LAVERY   No.

MAC   Well ... it's been a month. Knew it was bound ta happen sometime.

LAVERY   You can't say anything, Mac. The official word will be given in a few hours.

MAC   Right. Oh! I'm on ta you Captain. Is that why ya came ta see me last night on watch? Fer a wee bit.

LAVERY   Yes.

MAC   I wish I'd known. Was it yer idea, David?

LAVERY   Wha?

MAC   Ta push back? Did they listen ta ya?

LAVERY   Yes, they did. They asked my opinion. We had no choice.

MAC   A' course no. Good move, sir.

LAVERY   Mac. I could talk to Donaldson. Say that I need you here to assist me with...

MAC   Don't you bloody dare, David. What we da' is one thing. But it's no why I'm here. If I'm goin', I'm goin.

LAVERY   Yes. If the initial push is successful you'll

be back in a few days. I'll see you then.

MAC   Looking forward to it.

LAVERY   Private?

MAC   Sir?

LAVERY   Keep your head down.

                  MAC smiles.

MAC   I'll do my best.

                  LAVERY exits.

                  *Lights shift to Scotland. As MARY leads
                  DAVID past MAC. Who becomes TOM.
                  TOM joins at the end.*

MARY   It's no far now. Just up under Kingston
                  Bridge and there's a path doon ta the
                  river.

DAVID   Will Esther be alright?

TOM   She'll have some toffee. She'll be fine.

DAVID   You're a lively family. I'll give you that.

MARY   Oh yer Mum can push my pedals son.
                  What a sight we must seem ta' ya, Mr.
                  Lavery.

DAVID   Not to worry, Mary.

MARY   I'm so glad you could come, Mr. Lavery.
                  Da' didny ha' many pals. He'd been fair
                  chuffed.

DAVID   Thank you for your call, Mary

MARY   Oh ma pleasure. Well no a pleasure ... .

Oh Mr. Lavery! I swear sometimes mi heed button up the back. I've got yer letters ta Da'. I thought you might like ta hay them back.

> *MARY hands DAVID a bundle from her purse.*

DAVID   Thank you. Did you read them?

MARY   Oh ... just a few.

> *MARY smiles at DAVID and TOM and leads the way off. We see ESTHER wandering alone behind them. She exits.*
>
> *MARY leads DAVID and TOM further up the Clyde.*

TOM   This is the Clyde?

MARY   Oh aye, luv. You wern'y expecting heather, was ya?

TOM   Maybe be a little.

MARY   Further north is nicer.

DAVID   This area was heavily bombed during the war. The Clydebank blitz.

MARY   Aye. It's just us the auld shipyards doon here the now...

TOM   It's Hamilton.

MARY   We'd still swim in the summer sometimes...

DAVID   Yes. Mac mentioned that.

MARY   Let's keep goin'. Just a wee bit further.

> *MARY, TOM and David wander the river bank. We see that ESTHER is following them.*
>
> *They arrive at the side of the bridge.*

MARY Maybe this is fine. Oh I don't know ... maybe just a wee bit further.

TOM Was he any more specific?

MARY On the banks of the Clyde in a southbound wind.

Oh he ... he said something about the rock's...

> *DAVID moves a little further and is drawn to a specific spot.*

DAVID It's here, Mary.

> *DAVID has found some rocks on the shore. MARY walks to him.*

MARY Oh, Mr. Lavery, this is perfect. Now south...?

DAVID Directly this way ... actually five more degrees.

TOM I won't argue with that.

> *They all match DAVID's angle.*

TOM What do we do now?

> *MARY takes a concertina accordion out of her bag.*

MARY I'll just play him a wee tune first.

> *She plays "Scotland the Brave" ESTHER*

*comes into view behind. MARY senses
her presence.*

MARY   I thought you might find us, Esther.

ESTHER   I'll know that sound to my grave. Look at that water. The colour of urine — disgusting.

DAVID   You're just in time, Esther.

ESTHER   Oh am I? Lucky for me. Look at yeahs. A happy little group on a damp riverbank.

TOM   Esther! Go back to the house.

ESTHER   Aye. Look. There's yer Da' in ya. I see him in ya now. Oh yes. The same snarl. Stupid, stupid man.

TOM   It's too late. I don't want to know anymore.

ESTHER   Once. That's all it took, Tom! Parked down here. In his Mini. Slam bam. Then pregnant. Then married. Then you screamin' yer fool heed aff.

MARY   An' ya loved him, Esther. Dinny forget that part.

ESTHER   Aye. I did. I did. I had my sights set higher but I couldny' help mysel'.

MARY   Ya used ta dance for him at the pub. Yer kilt a little too short. Callum throwin' coins at yer feet.

ESTHER   Aye. Aw luvey dovey at first. He was a thug but he had a bit a' poetry in him. I caught him puttin' whiskey in your milk to help you sleep. You were headed the same way.

Then he was deed. Kilt by his own stu-
pidity. So I left. I cleaned the slate. So
what? That's why ya leave.

Silence.

ESTHER   I do remember you, Mr. Lavery.

DAVID   Yes, Esther.

ESTHER   Yes. Do you, Mary?

MARY   Oh, aye. Perfectly. The Copthorne Hotel
             Dining Room fer dinner. I was ten, you
             fourteen. Da's army buddy takin' us oot
             on the toon. We stayed the night afore wi
             Auntie Panty. Ya permed my hair.

ESTHER   We took a taxi to the hotel. We came in
             the front doors ... marble pillars. Into the
             dining room and there you were. Very
             distinguished as you still are.

MARY   A yellow shirt. Crystal chandelier right
             oer' the table.

ESTHER   Yes. A violinist in the corner.

DAVID   Yes. Two beautiful girls. I remember you
             both very well. Wee, shy Mary with your
             frizzy hair. And Esther the dancing star.
             Your toe in a bandage.

TOM   Your toe?

ESTHER   Yes.

TOM   That story's about you?

ESTHER   Sliced off during a moment of careless-
             ness. I never danced in competition again.
             It makes you really appreciate your toes.

DAVID   Mac was so worried about you.

ESTHER   Yes. You and Da' talked about the war.
               Then, after dessert, you started to whis-
               per. You were involved in a very serious
               discussion but I couldn't hear what you
               were saying. I tried. And then Da' said,
               "Oh no, David ... it's no possible". The
               way your eyes stayed on each other. I got
               a chill. Then you laughed and put your
               hand on top of his. Then rubbed it a little.
               His eyes sparkled. I hadn't seen that since
               ... Mum.

MARY   I'd never seen it.

ESTHER   I know, Mr. David.

TOM   Know what?

ESTHER   What I know. I just wanted you to know I
               knew. I'm not a stupid woman.

TOM   What?

ESTHER   He's the way you are. Your way.

TOM   And Mac?

ESTHER   Was his pal. I think that was nice of him.

TOM   Yes.

DAVID   I don't know what to say, Esther.

ESTHER   There's nothing to say, Mr. David. I think
               it best if we skirt the issue.

DAVID   Your father was a wonderful and brave
               man.

ESTHER   Yes.

TOM   What were you and Mac whispering
                   about David?

DAVID   What?

TOM   At the table?

DAVID   Oh it was a long time ago, Tom.

TOM   We want to know.

MARY   I canny say I'm no curious.

DAVID   I wanted Mac and his two wee girls to
                   come and live with me in Edinburgh. I
                   had all these rooms to fill. It seemed per-
                   fect ... but he wouldn't risk it. These wee
                   girls were his life, Tom.

                   Silence.

ESTHER   I was going to read some verse at the
                   service. But it seemed pointless...

MARY   Go ahead, pet.

ESTHER   No. I want you to read it, Mary. You did
                   put the day together. And I was thinking,
                   even before your tantrum, that you
                   should be the one to read it.

MARY   Are ya sure?

ESTHER   Yes, I'm sure.

                   *ESTHER opens her book of verse and
                   hands it to MARY.*

MARY   Oh a wee bit a' Burns. Lovely choice,
                   Esther.

ESTHER   Let's gather round. Mr. David ... right
                   here. Your medals will catch the light.

Tom, I think dance posture is appropriate.
Just the high-lighted and breath-barred
section.

MARY   What tho' on hamely fare we dine
              Wear hodden-grey an a' that:
              Gie fools their silks, and knaves their
              wine
              A man's a man for a' that.
              Our toils obscure an a' that.
              Their tinsel show, and a' that:
              The honest man tho' e'er sae poor,
              Is king o' men for a' that.

              Then let us pray that come it may
              as come it will for a' that,
              That sense and worth o'er the earth,
              Shall bear the gree for a' that,
              That man to man, the world o'er,
              Shall brithers be for a' that.

DAVID   Lovely.

ESTHER   We should scatter now. Southerly?

MARY   Yes. That's right, Esther.

ESTHER   Who should do the honours?

MARY   Here ya go, Esther.

              She hands the urn to ESTHER.

ESTHER   No Mary. You. You've got a stronger arm.

MARY   No Esther ... it's what Dad would have
              wanted. His dancing girl to fling him into
              the Clyde.

ESTHER   Really?

DAVID   That sounds perfect.

MARY	Oh yes, luv. You should have seen him, Tom. Every competition ... first row.
ESTHER	Yes. My dear sweet Da'. We'll finish this then we'll go home.
TOM	You see ... this is where I get confused. I thought we were home. When are we home?
ESTHER	I don't know.
	Tom. You're my home. You know that.
TOM	Yes.

ESTHER and MARY kneel to put the ashes in the Clyde. As the ashes float away TOM leans in and kisses DAVID.

Young CAPTAIN LAVERY enters.

LAVERY	Mac?

TOM turns to young LAVERY.

LAVERY	Mac?

TOM looks back to DAVID.

DAVID	Go on.

TOM turns and goes to young LAVERY. TOM is now MAC. Lights dim on ESTHER and MARY. DAVID watches over this scene in the desert.

MAC	Captain Lavery.
LAVERY	Mac. Where the hell have you been you wee bastard?

MAC   Hell. Did I no tell ya? I was on a wee hol-
iday.

LAVERY   I've been looking for you. Trust you to be
the last back.

MAC   Yer shakin' like a leaf, Captain. Did you
think I was a ghost?

                        *At this point, both DAVID and LAV-
ERY, the two personas of the same char-
acter, talk with MAC.*

DAVID   Yes.

LAVERY   There were so many loses. Lancaster said
he saw you carrying some injured men
back to the transports then he lost track
of you. I thought you were gone.

MAC   Not ta worry. I'm still kickin'.

DAVID   It's good to see you.

MAC   Yer plan was brilliant, Captain. The
Jerry's are on the run.

LAVERY   Yes a success by all accounts. Mac.
They're movin' me out tonight.

MAC   Wha'?

LAVERY   I'm off to HQ to observe.

MAC   What about the rest of us?

LAVERY   You're moving camp forward in the
morning.

MAC   Bloody hell! Have we still got a wee bit a
time.

DAVID   Aye ... a wee bit.

MAC   Well ... then I guess we could uh ... wrestle?

LAVERY   Yes.

They kiss passionately.

MAC   You coulda shaved!

LAVERY   Sorry.

They resume kissing. LAVERY's hands go up MAC's kilt.

LAVERY   Damn! I wish I had my kilt.

They kiss again.

LAVERY   Write when we get back. A wee note to tell me when I can see you. I can come down to Glasgow ... ..

MAC   It'll have to be a while. The wedding, work ... a year at least.

LAVERY   Just a note here and there ... Oh Jesus!

MAC   What?

LAVERY   It's just sand.

MAC   It's a'right.

They resume kissing.

MAC   I don't want ya ta go.

LAVERY   No. It was far too brief, Private. Just promise me you'll look after yourself, Mac. Come out in one piece.

MAC   Aye. I will. It'll be nice to gei hame. A regular life ... eh ... day to day ... know what

yer dain'. Maybe a bairn or two. Ah,
David ... the Clyde runs near my house ...
it's beautiful. Under Kingston Bridge.

DAVID   I know.

MAC   I'll take you there. Show it to you. I'll
leave my clothes beside the bridge just
when the sun's waning. I'll follow the
high rocks a little into the water then lie
down with the current rushing over me,
looking at the stars. It feels sa good ... I
get a wee bit scared.

LAVERY   I know.

DAVID breaks away.

DAVID   Mac. They're waiting for me. I better go.

MAC   Aye.

*LAVERY goes to leave but, before he
exits, he turns to look at MAC. DAVID
simply watches this scene.*

TOM   Safe journey.

*As LAVERY exits, music of the pipes
fades in and TOM assumes a Highland
dance position, arms raised. On his first
leap, lights go to black.*

The End.